3706

Jane Fonda

Jane Fonda
more than a movie star

Ellen Erlanger

 Lerner Publications Company ▪ Minneapolis

For Nana, who knew in her heart that I could

LIBRARY OF CONGRESS CATALOGING IN PUBLICATION DATA

Erlanger, Ellen.
Jane Fonda, more than a movie star.

(The Achievers)
Summary: A biography of the actress whose political
activities and publishing ventures have kept her constantly
in the public eye.
1. Fonda, Jane, 1937- Juvenile literature. 2. Moving-
picture actors and actresses — United States — Biography —
Juvenile literature. [1. Fonda, Jane, 1937-
2. Actors and actresses] I. Title. II. Series.
PN2287.F56E74   1984   791.43′028′0924 [B]   83-27542
ISBN 0-8225-0485-5 (lib. bdg.)

Manufactured in the United States of America

International Standard Book Number: 0-8225-0485-5
Library of Congress Catalog Card Number: 83-27542

1 2 3 4 5 6 7 8 9 10 93 92 91 90 89 88 87 86 85 84

JANE FONDA: MORE THAN A MOVIE STAR

Jane was in perfect costume for a Western. Dressed in cowboy hat and boots with blue jeans and flannel shirt, she made an ideal good guy. Her brother, Peter, liked to play the villain and imitated the outlaws he had seen in the movies.

Jane and Peter Fonda had plenty of space for acting out their make-believe films. They lived on a sprawling piece of property tucked in the hills above Hollywood, California. Their New England-style farmhouse, marked 900 Tigertail Road, had been designed by the children's parents, Frances and Henry Fonda.

Henry Fonda in one of his earliest films, *The Farmer Takes a Wife* (1934), co-starring Janet Gaynor

6

It was Henry Fonda's success as an actor that had helped to make the estate possible. Fonda, who had grown up in Nebraska, loved to farm. So along with the tennis court, playground, and life-size playhouse for the children, Henry had planted crops and certain favorite trees for his own pleasure. He also added animals: pet donkeys for Jane and Peter, plus three dogs, a cat, and many rabbits and chickens. Henry had even disguised a swimming pool to look like a farm pond.

The Fondas spent many happy days on Tigertail Road. But today, more than 35 years later, Jane Fonda has achieved her own success, and her life now is quite different from her childhood. A great deal has happened to Jane since she and Peter roamed the fields and foothills around their home. In everything she has done as an adult, Jane Fonda has proved to be a strong individual—not just the daughter of a famous person.

Although Jane Fonda is her own person, Henry Fonda's great talent certainly influenced her. So to better understand Jane, it is worthwhile to learn about her father.

Henry's success as an actor did not come easily. In fact, he didn't show much interest in acting until he had reached the age of 20. Before that, Henry—

or Hank, as he was called—had planned to become a writer. When he finished high school in 1923, Hank had left Nebraska to study journalism at the University of Minnesota. But in 1925, he quit school and returned home. He had decided that writing wasn't for him after all, but he really didn't know what he wanted to do.

Soon after returning to Omaha, a family friend urged Hank to try out for a play at the Omaha Community Playhouse. Hank had nothing better to do, so he finally agreed to try out. And because he didn't have much competition, he got the part. Most of the people who saw Hank's performance were not especially impressed. But some said that he had a special quality onstage, and they saw a spark of talent.

Hank must have sensed something, too, for with that first role he became hooked on the theater. He hung around the playhouse for two seasons and showed a willingness to work. Sometimes he acted, and other times he designed and painted scenery.

After a few summers of experience in other theaters in the Midwest, Hank left for New York in 1928 to try to carve out an acting career. He arrived in early summer, and not many jobs were available at that time. So Hank decided to try Cape Cod instead, where he knew several summer theaters were operating.

Hank joined a group of college students known as

the University Players Guild. At that time, he had no idea that some of these people would become his lifelong friends. Nor did he know that these actors, including James Stewart, Joshua Logan, and Mildred Natwick, would later become world-famous stars. And one of the actresses there, Margaret Sullavan, later became Henry Fonda's first wife.

At the end of the summer, Hank's acting friends all returned to college. So Hank went to New York as he had first planned to do. He struggled there for six years and barely made a splash. A series of unsuccessful roles kept him fairly close to hunger.

The turning point in Fonda's career came in 1934. A man named Leland Hayward saw Hank act and offered to become his agent. Almost overnight, Hayward arranged a movie contract for Hank with Hollywood producer Walter Wanger. Under the contract, Fonda could earn $1,000 a week making films. Though he had never thought of himself as a screen actor, Hank knew the offer was too good to refuse.

One of his movie roles in 1936 involved a trip to Europe. Fonda, divorced from Margaret Sullavan by then, met a young American widow, Frances Seymour Brokaw. The couple married in September, and the following April, Frances learned she was pregnant.

The baby was born December 21, 1937, in New York City. She was named Jane Seymour Fonda

Newlyweds Henry Fonda and Frances Seymour Brokaw following their marriage in 1936

to show the family roots of both parents. These roots gave the baby a lively political heritage. Fonda was an Italian name, and one of Henry's ancestors had led a struggle for freedom in Italy. The Seymours had their political connections, too. They were related to John and Samuel Adams, the 18th-century American rebel leaders. And much earlier, Lady Jane Seymour had married England's King Henry VIII.

For that reason, the Fondas nicknamed their new baby Lady Jane. She soon showed them, however, that she would rather be a tomboy than a lady. She rode horses from the age of five and sometimes started fights with the boys at the stables. Even after she broke her wrist while skating down the hall at home, she preferred roller skates to party shoes. Jane also wanted to wear clothes that resembled her father's movie costumes, though she couldn't figure out why he wore so many different outfits.

At home, Henry Fonda didn't talk much about his acting jobs. His wife was more interested in the world of business than in films and plays. Besides, it was Fonda's nature to keep to himself a lot. So it's no wonder that one day Jane asked, "Why can't Daddy make up his mind about his beard? First he lets it grow, then he shaves it off, then he grows it again!" Jane was too young to understand the difference between her father as an actor and her father as a dad.

In 1940 Henry appeared in *The Grapes of Wrath*, often thought of as the finest film performance of his career.

But as she grew older, Jane realized she was the daughter of a famous man. Her brother, Peter, who was born in 1940, could see this, too, especially when the family traveled with Hank on many of his film and theater trips.

The Fondas moved to Greenwich, Connecticut, shortly after Hank opened in Broadway's *Mister Roberts*, one of his most famous roles, in 1948. On opening night—the first of more than 11,000 performances—people stood on their seats at the end of the play, cheering on and on. Finally Fonda said, "This is all Tom and Josh (the authors) wrote for us. If you want, we can start all over again." In his review, one critic answered, "I hung around awhile, hoping they would."

But Jane and Peter were not so anxious to hang around in the East. They preferred their home on Tigertail Road, and they liked school better in California, too. It also seemed to them that their mother had been more relaxed out West.

Jane and Peter were right about this. Their mother had become increasingly unhappy through the years, especially while living in the East. Early in 1950, she placed herself in the care of a mental health facility, and she died there a few months later. It was not until they were older that Jane and Peter found out their mother had taken her own life.

The Fonda family in 1955. Henry's third wife, Susan Blanchard, whom he married in 1950, holds their adopted daughter, Amy.

Luckily, Jane and Peter became fond of their father's third wife, Susan Blanchard. She helped Jane build self-confidence, especially during her teenage years.

Naturally, Jane's classmates and teachers kept begging her to try acting. But she was reluctant to step onstage just because she was Henry Fonda's daughter. "I never wanted to follow in his steps," she recalls from the early years. Jane finally did agree to appear in a few high school plays. In her first role, she was cast as a boy, not unusual at an all-girls' school.

That role did not sell Jane on acting the way her father's first part had sold him on his career. As her 16th birthday approached in 1953, Jane had other ideas for herself. She planned to enter Vassar College in New York to study ballet or art.

In 1955, after Jane's first year at Vassar, her aunt Harriet invited her to appear with Henry in a summer production in Omaha. The play, *The Country Girl*, helped raise money for the same playhouse that had helped Henry Fonda get his start. The production was a real family affair—even Peter helped out by working backstage.

Jane was enthusiastic about her performance that summer, and her father was very proud of her. He had never tried to push her into acting, but he knew she had talent. In one scene, for instance, she had to walk onstage crying, a difficult task even for experienced performers. After she had handled the scene with ease and great feeling, she asked her father innocently, "How'd I do?" Fonda later told an interviewer, "She didn't understand that she'd done what many professionals couldn't do in a lifetime."

The next summer, Henry and Jane Fonda acted together again, this time in *The Male Animal* in Cape Cod, Massachusetts. But Jane still didn't seem interested in acting as a career. Her second year at Vassar hadn't pointed her toward a profession, either. She told her father she wanted to study art in Paris instead.

In part because he loved art himself, Fonda agreed to the idea. His own paintings had often sold for thousands of dollars, and greeting card companies had asked him to send in his designs. So Henry didn't mind helping his daughter get training in France, where she enrolled at L'Ecole de la Chauvière.

Once Jane started, however, she didn't work as hard as her father had expected. He suggested she return to New York City and enroll in classes there instead. She came back and registered at the Art Students League. At the same time, she dabbled in many other interests, including music, modeling, and foreign languages. In fact, by 1958 Jane was studying just about everything *but* acting. She did want to try it, but she was scared. What if Henry Fonda's daughter failed?

At age 18, Jane appeared with her father in *The Male Animal*. Here they relax during a rehearsal break.

Jane, Peter, and Henry board a plane bound for Europe. Jane was 19 years old when this photo was taken.

18

Toward the end of 1958, Jane and Peter Fonda joined their father in California. They lived at his Malibu beach house while he made a movie. During her stay at the beach, Jane became friendly with a young actress named Susan Strasberg. The two had met briefly the year before when Susan had appeared in her first movie, *Stage Struck*, with Jane's father.

Both of Susan's parents were acting coaches. Her father, Lee, was especially well known for running the Actors Studio in New York and for giving private acting lessons. Her mother, Paula, worked with some of America's top performers.

Susan Strasberg and some of her friends suspected that Jane Fonda was more interested in acting than she admitted, so they convinced her to give it a try. Lee Strasberg interviewed Jane and accepted her as a private student. He said a certain expression in her eyes convinced him that she would be able to act out many emotions if she took her training seriously.

Fonda moved to New York and attended Strasberg's classes twice a week for two hours at a time. But she devoted many more hours than that to her new career. In preparation for stage work, she also took ballet and modern dance instruction. And to pay for her lessons with Strasberg, she took up modeling again.

Jane was in great demand as a model, receiving $50 an hour. As early as July 1959, she appeared on the cover of *Vogue* magazine. Within months, people saw her face on the covers of several other major magazines as well.

Jane could have been very successful as a full-time model, but acting was more important to her than modeling. She worked hard to master "The Method" that Strasberg taught. This was an approach to acting that had been developed by a Russian director named Konstantin Stanislavski. "The Method" encouraged actors to experience, rather than imitate, the characters they were playing. Henry Fonda had never placed great value in "The Method," but his daughter followed the style closely.

Learning "The Method" was not easy for Jane. A staff member under Strasberg remembers, "She was like a frightened deer...the poor girl really felt quite out of place. But she had something." People in Omaha had once seen that same "something" in Henry Fonda, too.

About a month after signing up with Strasberg, Jane demonstrated that she was making progress. She went through the studio's onstage exercise, which was a series of physical movements and pantomimes. Afterward Strasberg told her, "You've got talent."

Fonda recalls Strasberg's encouragement with enthusiasm. "That was it...I went to bed excited about what I was doing, and I woke up and worked twice as hard as anybody else, just so nobody could say I was riding on my father's shirttails. It changed my life. Totally."

Studying under Strasberg certainly did change Jane's life. By the end of 1959, she had acted professionally on both stage and screen. Jane performed in a summer theater production of *The Moon Is Blue*, her first performance without her father. And Joshua Logan signed her to a movie contract.

Logan first cast Jane in *Tall Story* (1960), in which she played a college cheerleader in love with a basketball star acted by Anthony Perkins. Because of all the publicity she received before the film came out, people definitely noticed Jane. But the movie itself was not a great success.

Jane was aware that she was being treated differently because of her father's success and his connections, but she was anxious to establish her own reputation as a performer. "Contacts can get you there," she said, "but they won't keep you there. I'm planning to stay on my own."

Back in New York, Jane proved she meant what she said. Although her father was in the same city, he was busy with a Broadway play of his own. While his name was in lights for *Silent Night, Lonely Night*, Jane's name lit the marquee of *There Was a Little Girl*. A critic from the *New York Times* wrote,

"Although Miss Fonda looks a great deal like her father, her acting style is her own."

Jane's style alone couldn't save a sinking play, however. *Little Girl* lasted only 16 performances, but Fonda's stage career had been launched. In 1960 she appeared in *Invitation to a March*. A reviewer from *Newsday* said she had "a glow that almost dims the moonlight" and called her "surely the loveliest and most gifted of all our new actresses." Appropriately, she was named Most Promising New Actress by the New York Drama Critics that year.

With a few Broadway openings under her belt, Jane returned to the cameras of Hollywood. Her role in *A Walk on the Wild Side* (1962) was much more serious and demanding than other film parts she had played. So was her part in *The Chapman Report*, another 1962 film. Director George Cukor shared the enthusiasm of people who had seen Fonda in New York. "The only thing she has to watch," he said, "is that she has such an abundance of talent she must learn to hold it in. She is an American original."

Jane finally seemed to be off and running in a career she enjoyed. By late 1962, she already had several accomplishments to her credit. Yet in spite of her success, she had reasons for unhappiness as well. Two close friends had recently committed suicide. And her relationship with her father had become rocky. The two Fondas exchanged jabs through the press. Part of the tension came from their disagreement over Andreas Voutsinas, an acting coach. Jane's father strongly objected to the way Voutsinas seemed to be controlling Jane's career. In the end, Jane herself realized that she needed to handle her affairs more independently.

By 1963 Jane had settled many of her personal problems. The Actors Studio, which had accepted Jane two years before, presented a revival of the play *Strange Interlude*. In this play, Jane had the chance to act with some of her idols, such as actress Geraldine Page. Soon afterward she enjoyed playing the comical leading lady in the film *Sunday in New York*.

At about this time, filmmakers in other countries, especially in France, began to notice Jane. She went there to act in the film *Joy House* and was then signed by director Roger Vadim for *La Ronde (Circle of Love)*. Jane and Vadim became very close while they worked together on the film, and they were married in 1965.

That year Jane appeared in her first big hit film, *Cat Ballou*. Two other comedies, *Any Wednesday* (1966) and *Barefoot in the Park* (1967), followed closely. Her leading man in *Barefoot* was another rising star, Robert Redford.

Meanwhile, Jane had not given up on more serious

Cat Ballou was Jane's first big hit. In this Western spoof, she co-starred with Dwayne Hickman *(left)*, Michael Callan *(right)*, Lee Marvin, and Nat King Cole.

roles. In 1967 director Otto Preminger chose her for *Hurry Sundown*, and she played opposite Marlon Brando in another serious film, *The Chase*. Her husband continued to cast her in widely varied films as well. She starred in *The Game Is Over*, a serious, dramatic movie, and in *Barbarella*, a comedy set in the future, in which Jane's character was based on a French comic strip heroine. Because Fonda appeared in certain scenes wearing very little clothing, she was labeled a sex symbol by many moviegoers. That term had been used to describe her in other movie roles, too.

Jane and her first husband, Roger Vadim, at the Rome airport in 1967

In 1968, however, the name-calling eased for a while. Fonda temporarily left filmmaking because she was pregnant and wanted to prepare seriously for parenthood. On September 28, 1968, Vanessa Vadim was born, and it was a very special day for her mother. Jane recalls, "For the first time in my life, I felt comfortable as a human being and as a woman....I began to feel a unity with people. I began to love them.... When she was born, it was as if the sun had opened up for me."

And in many ways, perhaps it had. Jane Fonda was about to enter a new, active period in her life, and not just as a mother. Her greatest movie roles were yet to come, as well as many important new roles in the world of politics.

In 1969 reviewer Pauline Kael predicted that Jane Fonda would dominate movies in the 1970s. And most critics agree that that decade of filmmaking was Jane's finest to date.

Kael made this prediction after the release of *They Shoot Horses, Don't They?* In that movie, Jane played the part of Gloria, a bitter young woman who entered a dance marathon contest in the 1930s. Jane knew the role of Gloria would be a difficult one, so she decided to do everything she could to experience her character's emotions. She read books about the Depression, the time in which the story took place,

Fonda and Susannah York during a scene from *They Shoot Horses, Don't They?* York received an Oscar nomination for her role in the film.

and talked with people who had lived through it. Fonda took her preparation so seriously that other people thought that she had really "become" Gloria for a while.

The film included many exhausting scenes, so Jane had to be in top physical condition. She jogged along the beach for an hour every day. She also swam regularly and went on a strength-building diet. It's a good thing she was in shape, for as she recalls, "When we finished the endurance race sequences, everybody would collapse, weeping hysterically....It was the toughest thing I've had to do—ever."

The hard work paid off, though. Jane received the New York Film Critics Award for best actress of 1969 and was also nominated for an Oscar that year. In 1971 Jane starred as Bree Daniel in the thriller *Klute*. Again she did a great deal of extra work to prepare herself for the role. She talked with people in New York who lived like Bree, and they showed her some very unpleasant conditions. But they also helped her perform so realistically that she won the Oscar for best actress.

A 1973 film production of Henrik Ibsen's well-known play *A Doll's House* starred Jane as the character Nora, a strong, rather liberated woman. This was a fitting role for Fonda, and her portrayal was excellent.

Talking with people on the streets of New York City helped Jane prepare for her role as a call girl in *Klute*.

While Jane was enjoying several film successes, Peter, too, was busy. His controversial 1969 film *Easy Rider* grossed $25 million.

In 1976 Jane returned to comedy as George Segal's wife in *Fun with Dick and Jane*. The next year, Jane received an Oscar nomination for her role in *Julia*. In this film, Jane portrayed author Lillian Hellman in a true story based on Hellman's personal and political experiences as a young woman.

As usual, Fonda worked hard to "become" the character she was portraying. She began reading one of Hellman's most famous plays but stopped in the middle of the second act. Then she finished writing the play herself, as if *she* were Lillian Hellman. It was no wonder that Fonda's performance was so convincing.

Following *Julia*, many films were produced by Jane's own company, IPC Films, Inc., which she formed with her friend Bruce Gilbert. Their first project was *Coming Home* (1978), for which Jane won her second Oscar. This powerful film showed the effects of the Vietnam War upon the characters. Jane had very strong feelings about this war and knew many people who had fought in it, so she took the subject especially seriously and was able to give a most effective performance.

Fonda's feelings about the Vietnam War were expressed through her portrayal as the wife of a Marine captain (Bruce Dern) in *Coming Home*.

Jane's next starring role was in *Comes a Horseman* with James Caan and Jason Robards. In this film, Fonda portrayed a tough Western woman struggling to save her ranch. As always, she wanted to give a convincing performance, so she hired Colorado ranch hands to teach her their trade. In a short time, she was practically an expert ranch boss. Director Alan Pakula praised her as an expert actress, too. He said she was capable of playing a greater range of characters than any star of her generation.

Also in 1978, Fonda co-starred with Alan Alda in the Neil Simon comedy *California Suite*. Meanwhile, she was preparing the role of Kimberly Wells, a TV reporter thrown into the midst of a nuclear accident. *The China Syndrome*, which also starred Jack Lemmon and Michael Douglas, was a critical and box office sensation—even before the event at Three Mile Island in Pennsylvania paralleled the film accident and alarmed the world. For her performance, Jane won an Oscar nomination for the third straight year.

The China Syndrome (1979) was a Michael Douglas-IPC Films Production, and Jane contributed many of the key ideas. Douglas, Fonda, and Gilbert hoped to turn out a good thriller. But they also wanted audiences to consider the vast powers of corporations and the possible dangers of nuclear energy. These messages came through very successfully.

In *The China Syndrome*, Michael Douglas played the role of a TV cameraman, and Fonda, a news reporter covering an accident at a nuclear power plant.

In 1980 in *The Electric Horseman*, Fonda again co-starred with Robert Redford. In her next film, Jane starred with Lily Tomlin and Dolly Parton in *Nine to Five*, an IPC comedy about secretaries. Intensive talks with working women gave Fonda and Bruce Gilbert many ideas for this film, which took a good look at women's roles in American office life. As always, Jane's purpose with this film was to convey serious social messages as well as to entertain. And her 1981 film *Rollover* also had a political theme: corruption in the world of international high finance.

Jane Fonda and Lily Tomlin in a scene from *Nine to Five*

Heiress Lee Winters (Fonda) and banker Hub Smith (Kris Kristof-ferson) are two sophisticated, glamorous characters in *Rollover*.

Many of Fonda's movies have presented provocative messages, and some of these messages have angered people. But Fonda has never been afraid to work on controversial films. "You can be a privileged movie star," she has said, "or you can commit yourself to the idea that people can change their lives and can change history. I want to make films that will make people feel stronger, understand more clearly, and make them move forward—women and men. That's what I'm interested in."

Jane Fonda's commitment to helping people has gone far beyond the ideas and characters she has represented in her films. Although her awareness of major issues surfaced strongly during the filming of *They Shoot Horses*, it was certainly not the first time Jane had questioned social issues. Several years earlier, during her marriage to Roger Vadim, Fonda had traveled to the Soviet Union, and she became aware of the different form of government there. She also spoke to many people in France about the complexities of the war in Vietnam. Although she usually defended the United States because it was her homeland, she soon began to question some of the nation's policies at home as well as abroad.

Jane found the struggles of Native Americans especially upsetting. Her interest in their cause had been sparked by Marlon Brando when the two appeared in *The Chase* in 1966. Jane was equally concerned about growing tensions between blacks and whites in the United States. She was horrified by the incidents she saw in Louisiana in 1967 during the filming of *Hurry Sundown*. Some white residents of the area objected because black actors had leading roles. The angry individuals slashed tires, made threatening phone calls, and protested the use of the motel pool by blacks. Such prejudice made Jane furious.

When Fonda returned to France after *Sundown*,

This scene in San Francisco typifies the peace marches that were taking place across the U.S. during the 1960s and early 1970s.

she kept close track of political events at home. She joined several marches with other critics of the Vietnam War. Although in 1968 her pregnancy kept her less physically active than usual, she remained well aware of the troubled times in the United States.

In the late 1960s, the headlines were filled with news of riots, assassinations, and antiwar protests. When she came back to the U.S. from France to film *Horses*, Jane knew that she would find her nation tense and unsettled, and indeed she did. Conditions in the United States were quite confusing, and they forced her to think more deeply than ever about many issues. So did the film itself. In the movie, Jane played a desperate person, a sort of victim of society. While she was portraying this character, Jane thought of other victims of society, both in the United States and throughout the world. Jane wondered how politics might help to improve these people's lives and decided to do her part by becoming even more directly involved in political activity.

When the filming of *Horses* was over, Jane wanted to sort out her thoughts. She believed this would be easier in a completely different setting, so she visited India. The trip did not give Fonda the peace of mind she was seeking, however. Instead it made her aware of the widespread hunger and conflict that existed in India. She came back to the United States more determined than ever to work for the kind of nation and world she wanted.

Fonda began by offering her help to the antiwar movement. She also contacted the author of a magazine article on Native American rights and asked him to escort her to a protest so that she could speak with Native American leaders there. These leaders were demanding that the old prison building at Alcatraz be turned into a university for Native Americans. They were listing other demands as well.

Jane Fonda's visit to Alcatraz attracted a great deal

of publicity, but she emphasized that she was *not* getting into politics for attention. She cared deeply about issues, and she wanted to learn more about them. "You can do one of two things," she said. "Just shut up, which is something I don't find easy, or learn an awful lot very fast, which is what I tried to do."

Fonda's concerns were not limited to the Native American problem. She also learned about the women's movement and the problems of welfare clients and migrant workers. She spoke to members of the Black Panthers and the Young Lords, a Puerto Rican organization. And she became closely associated with the GI Movement, which helped soldiers speak out against the war and any other military practices they opposed. In 1970 Jane visited many coffeehouses established by the GI Movement near army bases. She was arrested for these visits more than once.

Fonda, in fact, faced a number of legal problems in 1970. She was arrested while marching for Native American rights and teargassed while speaking for a bombing halt in Vietnam. She became more and more angry about the war there, especially when President Nixon ordered American troops to invade Cambodia, one of Vietnam's neighboring countries. Then in November 1970, customs officials at Cleveland Hopkins Airport arrested Jane and charged her with smuggling drugs from Canada. She later proved that

At this 1970 antiwar rally, Jane spoke to a crowd of nearly 4,000 students.

her pills were all vitamins, not illegal drugs, and that they had been bought in the United States before her trip began. Jane felt that she was being purposely mistreated by the officials. She suspected they were giving her a rough time because she had criticized the government so often.

Many people assumed that Jane Fonda was guilty when they heard about her arrest. After all, she had been the subject of controversy in the past. Although Fonda's films were usually very popular, her political views were not.

Nothing seemed to stop Jane from expressing her opinions, however. In 1971 she and her *Klute* co-star, Donald Sutherland, organized an antiwar variety show called "F.T.A."—short for Free the Army. They performed the show near army bases, trying to offer a different type of entertainment from the purely patriotic shows put on by the government. Later, F.T.A. won the off-Broadway Obie Award and was filmed by American International Pictures. Fonda and Sutherland also started a fundraising drive among celebrities who opposed the war. Barbra Streisand and Burt Lancaster were two of those who helped in this effort, called the Entertainment Industry for Peace and Justice.

As the 1972 Academy Awards ceremony approached, many wondered how Jane Fonda would behave while onstage to accept her award. Would she come at all? And if she did, would she try to use the stage for a political speech? The nominee herself thought carefully about this, and, after talking it over with her father, decided to treat the occasion like any other Oscar evening. So when she accepted her golden statue for *Klute*, Fonda simply told the crowd, "There's a lot I could say tonight. But this isn't the time or the place. So I'll just say—thank you."

Three months later, however, Fonda said a great deal more, and she said it in the capital of North

Jane with Gene Hackman at the 1972 Academy Awards ceremony. Fonda won her Oscar for *Klute*, and Hackman his for
The French Connection.

Vietnam. She arranged her secret journey to Hanoi
with the help of Tom Hayden, an antiwar leader she
had met just before the Oscars. When she arrived, she
spoke on the radio to American soldiers, telling them

the evils of the United States' involvement in the war. Many U.S. citizens and political figures believed she had gone too far with this form of protest. Some even called her a traitor.

Still, she and Hayden were fairly well received when they went on a speaking tour in the United States a few months later. In 90 cities across the country, they showed slides of Vietnam and spoke against President Nixon's policies there.

During the tour, Fonda and Tom Hayden decided to marry. Jane's marriage to Roger Vadim had fallen apart in recent years, but neither had officially ended it. Jane obtained a divorce from Vadim in January 1973 and married Hayden soon afterward.

In their years together, Fonda and Hayden have continually worked together for the causes in which they so strongly believe. They have devoted great energy to both long-term change and day-to-day demonstration. And they have tried to educate the public in a variety of ways—through speeches, articles, films, and through the efforts of an organization called the Campaign for Economic Democracy (CED), formed by Hayden in the mid-70s.

CED has supported a number of issues, including solar power, rent control, and the rights of women and minorities. The organization has strongly opposed nuclear power, war, and certain political figures.

Obviously, Fonda's films, especially *Coming Home* and *The China Syndrome*, have addressed many of the issues that Hayden's organization represents.

Hayden spoke frequently of these ideas when he ran for the U.S. Senate in 1976 on the California primary ballot. Very few political experts expected him to do well. But when the results were tallied, Tom Hayden had received over 40 percent of the vote.

Although he lost that election, Hayden remained active in politics, particularly in addressing energy issues. In 1979 he and Fonda toured over 50 cities, criticizing the use of nuclear power in the United States and urging the adoption of solar alternatives. There was still anger in many cities over the couple's earlier antiwar tactics, and sometimes they were threatened by bomb scares or angry demonstrators. And Fonda was rejected as a nominee for a post on the California Arts Council because her former activities were still resented.

Despite these difficulties, however, Fonda and Hayden generally drew large crowds on their tours. In late September 1979, they joined other speakers and entertainers at an antinuclear gathering of some 200,000 people in New York City. "We are here to propose a conversion program from a nuclear to a non-nuclear society," said Hayden. And he vowed to carry this message to as many other places as possible.

Fonda with her husband, Tom Hayden, at the Three Mile Island nuclear power plant in Pennsylvania. Both are outspoken opponents of nuclear energy.

Tom and Jane at swearing-in ceremonies before the start of the California legislature's 1983-84 session. With them is their 7-year-old son, Troy.

In 1982 Hayden was successful in his second run for political office when he won the election for California State Assemblyman in the 44th District. And Jane remained politically active, too. Together, Tom and Jane continued to commit themselves to important issues.

During certain periods of her life, Jane Fonda's

relationship with her father was strained. But late in Henry's life, their ties became closer than ever. In 1981 Jane starred with Henry in the movie *On Golden Pond*. Henry played the part of a difficult, cranky, retired college professor spending what might be his last summer at his family's cottage. Katherine Hepburn played Henry's wife, and Jane, their daughter.

Katherine Hepburn, Henry Fonda, and Jane Fonda in *On Golden Pond*

Jane had bought the rights to *On Golden Pond* especially so that she could appear in it with her father. The relationship of the two characters in the movie paralleled in many ways Henry and Jane's real-life relationship, and the filming of *On Golden Pond* was an emotional experience for both of them.

Henry Fonda won an Oscar for his performance in *On Golden Pond*, the first of his career. Unfortunately, his health was so poor that he was unable to attend the ceremony. Jane accepted the award for him.

An ailing Henry Fonda poses with Jane and his fifth wife, Shirlee Adams Fonda, after winning an Oscar for *On Golden Pond*. Henry and Shirlee were married in 1967.

Hank is congratulated by Peter, Jane, and Amy after a performance of his one-man show, *Clarence Darrow*, in Los Angeles. Fonda had had a pacemaker implanted five weeks earlier, when he collapsed after a performance in New York.

Henry's health had been failing since 1974, when he had a pacemaker inserted to help his serious heart condition. Despite his poor health, however, he had continued to work hard, appearing in several Broadway plays and television productions. For instance, his one-man performance as Clarence Darrow, a famous trial lawyer, was a Broadway smash. The strain of the two-hour performance, however, had caused total exhaustion.

Shirlee Fonda is comforted by Jane, Amy, and Peter as she talks with newspeople following Henry's death.

After the filming of *On Golden Pond*, Henry Fonda's condition became critical. On August 12, 1982, he died at the age of 77.

Henry had been pleased that his relationship with Jane had improved so much over the years. Though he hadn't always agreed with his daughter's methods of political protest, he was continually proud of her courage and dedication to the causes she supported.

Jane and Henry share a happy moment. Tensions between the two had lessened greatly during the final years of Henry's life.

After all, in earlier years he had expressed some unpopular views of his own.

Today Jane Fonda realizes that her father was "a very progressive person." He demonstrated this by signing petitions, supporting political candidates, and making important films. *The Grapes of Wrath* (1940), for example, was just one Henry Fonda film that dealt with human needs and suffering. Jane has called it a "perfect" movie.

As an actress, Jane Fonda has tried to make "perfect" movies of her own. In 1981, in fact, Fonda was named by the *New York Times* as the top female box-office attraction in the United States. But Fonda's goals go far beyond making great films and gaining popularity as a star. She carries out many other roles in her life today as well. Besides an accomplished actress, she is a wife, mother, producer, political organizer, and author, and she wants to show that all these roles can blend together smoothly. James Bridges, director of *The China Syndrome*, has said, "She is an absolute professional who has a life bigger than her career." As proof of this, Fonda was included as one of the world's 10 most admired women in 1980.

During the early 1980s, Fonda's career took a new path that proved both popular and lucrative. *Jane Fonda's Workout Book*, published in 1981, topped all nonfiction best-sellers during 1982 and stayed on the

At her exercise studio, Fonda directs participants in a "benefit workout" for the Equal Rights Amendment.

best-seller list for most of 1983. She also published *Jane Fonda's Workout Book for Pregnancy, Birth, and Recovery* (1982), another very successful venture. Thousands of tapes, records, and videos were sold to go along with these books. Jane has also written a book on fitness for older women. And to further her interest in physical fitness and nutrition, Fonda opened several exercise and health salons called "Workout" and has started her own line of exercise clothes.

Vanessa, Jane, Tom, and Troy in New York City, where Jane was filming *Rollover*.

Despite her many successes, Fonda's life is neither showy nor glamorous. She and Tom live in a simple frame house with Jane's daughter, Vanessa, and their own son, Troy, who was born in 1973. They drive a well-used car, and they do their own house chores.

"It's easy for me to say I don't want anything," Jane comments, "because I've had it all."

Both Jane and Tom know that not everyone in the United States has been as lucky as they have been. Besides helping the less fortunate through CED, they have set up a ranch outside of Santa Barbara, California, where political workers receive special training and low-income children attend camp. In some ways, the camp is like any other, with swimming, riding, and lessons in animal care. But the youngsters also build solar energy equipment and study California history from the viewpoint of the state's minority groups.

At the camp, creativity in many forms is encouraged. In fact, Vanessa has written, directed, and starred in many camp plays. Perhaps she will represent the next generation of the Fonda family in acting. Jane Fonda intends to let Vanessa and Troy make their own decisions about their futures, however. She believes, as did her father, that each individual should choose his or her own path in life.

When Jane was 23 years old, she acted on Broadway in *Invitation to a March*. The character she played, Norma Brown, received this advice from a lively older woman: "What I did, I did because it was right for me. There's a little bell inside that tells you what's right for you. When it rings, you open your door and *go*!"

Jane Fonda seems to have taken that advice seriously. For much of her life, she has been trying to discover what is right for her and which bell she should answer. Along the way, she has opened many doors, and some have failed to lead her to happiness. But now she seems to be aware of her goals. She has a sense of purpose, and she controls her own projects. Jane Fonda has become her own woman, a person with the courage to grow and change. Who knows what challenge she'll tackle next?

ACKNOWLEDGMENTS: The photographs are reproduced through the courtesy of pp. 1, 6, 12, 24, 27, 29, 30, 31, 33, 34, 35, 47, Collectors Book Store; pp. 2, 10, 14, 17, 18, 25, 37, 40, 42, 45, 46, 48, 49, 50, 51, 53, 54, Wide World Photos, Inc. Cover photographs courtesy of Collectors Book Store (color) and Wide World Photos, Inc. (b/w).